MW00441037

Understand and Break Free From Your Own Limitations

MATTHEW BRIGHTHOUSE

Copyright © 2017

Table of Contents

1
Introduction

By picking up this book, the chances are that you have taken the Briggs-Myers Personality Test, and you have come up as an ENTJ personality type. Congratulations! You are a rare breed indeed, and you are certainly a force to be reckoned with!

Some of the greatest businessmen and women, entrepreneurs and general go-getters on this planet are ENTJ personality types, but this type only makes up 3% of the general population. If you have come up with this result after taking the test, that means you are someone who is determined, dogged, and someone who loves to achieve and will stop at nothing until that achievement is complete. You are also someone who is fantastic at recognizing the talents and strengths of others, even when they don't see them themselves. This means that as a team leader, you are the ideal choice to motivate and ensure the team's success, whilst being an inspiration for others too.

Of course, every personality type has its upsides and downsides, and the ENTJ is no different. We will discuss your strengths and weaknesses in a bit more detail in our next chapter, but the ENTJ overall is someone who can be a little cold emotionally, simply because they are so focused on the end goal. It's not as though you choose to be this way, or that you even know you're doing it, it really is that you are so driven and determined, that half measures are not acceptable to you. The biggest challenge you will face through your self-development journey, as an ENTJ, will be the ability to tap into your emotions – but, it can be done!

The aim of this book is to help you recognize your strengths and develop them further, giving yourself a pat on the back for the sheer strength and will to succeed that you have, but also to help you recognize your weaknesses. The point of knowing where you fall short is that you can work to improve these, therefore developing yourself as a person. We all know we have short-comings, but it might be that you don't really know what yours are; by the end of this book you will understand them, and you will have the advice and tools to put into place, in order to change them into a positive. ENTJs love criticism, ironically, because they see it as a chance to grow – you could, therefore, argue that you already have the best mindset to carry forward your journey of personal development. Many others would dwell and internalize criticism, but not you!

It may also be that you have found you are an ENTJ personality type, but that you are also someone who displays traits of the surrounding types. It is unlikely that anyone is ever 100% a particular type because we are all individuals who have quirks and differences. It is, therefore, a great idea to read the book cover to cover of your main type, but then skim the others which you are displaying, to help you truly develop yourself to the maximum amount possible. It is also wise to not attach labels to ourselves. By being honest with yourself and digging a little deeper, you'll be able to recognize where you fall short.

So, are you ready to discover your true self as an ENTJ?

2
The Fine Line Between Strength and Weakness

We mentioned in our introduction section that an ENTJ is a true leader, a true force of nature who will stop at nothing to succeed. You were born to lead, it is in your DNA, and it is something you find that comes out of your personality, whether you want it to or not. The point here is that you need to embrace that leadership – you are an extrovert, you are someone who can inspire others to do great things!

The ENTJ is often referred to as 'The Commander', because of that leadership point. As an ENTJ, it is likely that you are very confident and charismatic, and you exude this charm effortlessly. You are able to pull people together to achieve a common outcome, and you are an excellent team leader as a result. People are drawn to you, you are somewhat of an enigma or a mystery, but you are also someone who is influential and inspiring, because of your hard work and determination.

ENTJs only make up a small fraction of the population, in fact just 3%. Some of the greatest business minds on the planet and in history were, or are, ENTJs; Bill Gates, Barack Obama, Steve Jobs, Margaret Thatcher, Jim Carrey, and Harrison Ford are names on that list. As you can see, we have some huge business names there – Bill Gates! You are of the same type as the great Bill Gates! A former US President, a former UK Prime Minister, two of the most flexible and talented actors on the planet. You are in good company. This list should bring to the fore the real drive and determination which really dominates the ENTJ type.

So, what does ENTJ stand for?

- Extraversion
- Intuition
- Thinking
- Judgement

Extraversion
You are no wallflower, and you are no shrinking violet. You are a go-getter, you are a speaker, you are a leader. You are happiest when you have the bit between your teeth and an aim to work towards, and you won't stop until that aim has been achieved. You truly believe that you can achieve anything if you put in the work, and that is a wonderful quality to have. Of course, the downside of that is that you can sometimes trample over others, unknowingly, in order to achieve your goal. This is something you can work towards and grow from.

Anyone who is more of an introvert, and therefore more sensitive or emotional, is not someone you understand, and that often means that you can hurt the feelings of those people quite easily. Of course, it is not that you mean to do so, it is simply that this is not your way. Learning to be more tolerant and understanding of the emotions of those around you is, therefore, a key improvement area that we will talk about in greater depth later on.

Intuition
Where business is concerned, you have a finely-honed sense of how to get where you want to be. This, of course, doesn't have to be business focused, it can be an aim that you are determined to tick off your list overall. Whilst you aren't really emotionally tuned, you focus more on the logic and hard work of an issue, which gets you successfully where you need to be in the end. As an ENTJ, it is your willpower, determination, and tuning into your intelligence, that really pushes you towards your goal.

Thinking
ENTJs are fantastic at thinking strategically, so if there is a problem that needs to be solved in a logical and successful (there's that word again) way, then an ENTJ is your man or woman. Sometimes this doesn't make you the most popular person around because you are forced to make difficult and sometimes ruthless decisions. For instance, in the case of Margaret Thatcher, the former UK Prime Minister. Mrs. Thatcher was not the most popular person, but she was dogged, determined, and she made hard decisions with a sharp brain when she had to. Love her or hate her, you can't deny her determination and will to succeed. You are the same in many ways because sometimes your decisions can alienate you, but you are someone who demands so much respect at the same time.

Judgement

Every single human being on the planet, whether ENTJ or otherwise, is judgemental to a degree. We are designed to be different, and we are all hard-wired to understand ourselves, but can often find it hard to understand others with more complex issues or types. As an ENTJ, you are someone who can be cold and ruthless at times, and as we mentioned before, if you are dealing with someone who is more emotional, you often don't handle the situation too well.

For instance, Simon Cowell isn't an ENTJ personality type per se, but he does exhibit many of the traits. Simon is known for his determination, and he is often so brutal with his feedback that he doesn't realize he is being hurtful of the feelings of others. Of course, underneath this, we know that he doesn't purposely set out to be hurtful, but that he has his own unique way of delivering what he perceives to be the truth or the right way to proceed. Underneath it all, he is actually quite soft, but doesn't allow his feelings to show – can you see the similarity? Not necessarily with Simon Cowell, but the behavior trait.

Okay, so we've covered what an ENTJ is at its very core, and you know that as this particular personality type, you are a rare and very driven breed. Let's now look at the main strengths and weaknesses. It's important to realize that this is not an exhaustive list, because we are all so individual as people. You may have another particular upside or downside, that isn't listed here, but overall, as the main features, you can certainly expect to display the following points to some degree or another.

Strengths of an ENTJ

- **ENTJs are efficient and hard-working**
  You will be hard-pressed to find a personality type who will work as hard and be as focused to achieve as an ENTJ. There is a huge amount of energy that goes into any venture here, and that means working extra hours and going over and above what is expected, in order to get where they need to be. Learning to balance all of that with personal time, however, is a key.

- **ENTJs are confident, charismatic, and charming**
  Barack Obama is an ENTJ, and he ticks this box perfectly. A truly charming, charismatic and self-assured, confident person, the former President can easily convince those around him, e.g. in public speaking, that his way is the right one. As an ENTJ, it is likely that you have this exuding charisma, which comes in very useful in presentations and meetings, and also succeeds in making many people look up to you.

- **ENTJs are extremely determined and strong willed**
  A little in line with our first point, an ENTJ has cast iron will, and that means they will stop at nothing to achieve their aim. This determination is dogged and extreme. Again, this is a great trait to have, but it is also something which can go over and above and can go into territory where that person doesn't give themselves 'off' time.

- ENTJs are fantastic at strategic thinking
  If you are looking for someone who is able to piece together the parts of a puzzle in a strategic way, in order to solve a problem or quandary, then an ENTJ is the right person for the job. This is someone who will stay up until late, will remain in the office when they should be at home, and someone who will brainstorm until they come up with the most innovative way to get around an issue. Again, we just mentioned it, but learning to create balance and harmony in life is also key.

- ENTJs are ideal team leaders
  We know that an ENTJ is a born leader, and they are also fantastic at picking the right people to work alongside them. ENTJs are great at recognizing the strengths of others, and can easily be a true inspiration to their team members. People look up to ENTJs, and they are fascinated by their determination and success. There is nothing more attractive than a successful person! Being able to see the hidden potential in team members is also something an ENTJ is very good at doing and makes them great in the recruitment world.

Weaknesses of an ENTJ

- ENTJs can be stubborn, cold, and sometimes ruthless

The downside of that determined spirit is that as an ENTJ, you can often come over to other people as being cold and ruthless. The greatest leaders, of course, do need to have this trait because this is often the only way to succeed. Again, we will cast our mind back to Margaret Thatcher. Stubbornness is also a common trait amongst ENTJs, and an unwillingness to back down or let go of an issue if something isn't working. It is likely that you don't even realize you are displaying this trait, and one of our chapters is going to talk about how to become a little more in tune with your emotions, and how to harness that determination for good.

- ENTJs can be overwhelming and over-dominant
  To an introverted or more emotional personality type, an ENTJ can be overwhelming, over-bearing, and over-dominant. This is often the price you pay for being a determined go-getter type of person, because in order to beat down barriers and succeed, you need to be in the faces of the people that need it. The key here is to know when to do this, and when to pull back. Again, we are going to talk in a specific chapter about how to achieve this, so you can call on your skill of being dominant when you need to be, but also recognize when to draw back a little and be softer.

- ENTJs can be intolerant
  One of the most common causes for concern when dealing with an ENTJ is that they can be insensitive quite easily. Again, this is not an

12

actual focus, it is not something that you, as an ENTJ, set out to do. Your focus and drive mean that you simply don't understand or have time for those who are more emotionally charged or those who like to 'go with the flow'. You can't get your head around it, because that is not the way you are hardwired. Again, learning how to recognize this weakness and address it will help you develop. It's also important to realize that the 'flow' can also lead to great places you may not have thought of!

- ENTJs can be impatient
  When a job is on the line, an ENTJ doesn't have time for dilly-dallying around! This impatient streak can push into situations away from work too. For instance, Jim Carrey is a top actor, someone who is supremely talented, but he is very impatient – look at all that nervous energy! Learning to stop, take time for yourself, and develop a home/life balance is key to helping yourself and those around you. This is also important when avoiding the burn out issue which we will talk about in more detail later in our book.

- ENTJs do not handle emotions well
  And now we have the main one, the one we have touched upon several times already. It isn't that an ENTJ is devoid of emotion. Far from it, it is just that when in a certain zone, e.g. at work or in situations where success is on the line, they do not process their feelings as well as someone who is more introverted, or in tune with what

they are feeling. Feelings are not as logical to you as an ENTJ, and a lot of the time you don't understand them, which causes you a lot of frustration. Not everyone is a truly emotional person, but we are going to talk in another chapter about how to not only be more tolerant of the feelings of others, but also how to get in tune with your own – you might even find that a more emotional approach to a problem could be a route to success.

As you can see, the ENTJ is a complex type indeed! You are a melting pot of success, drive, determination, inspiration, and occasional ruthlessness and insensitivity. Now, if you're ready to get practical, let's see how we can turn those weaknesses into positives, and develop you into an even bigger force to be reckoned with! Remember to keep an open mind with all the information we are going to give you, and to look at it from all sides, before deciding whether or not it is an area you need to work on, or not.

Remember, criticism and advice are not negative, they are a tool for growth.

3
Learn to be More Tolerant With The Feelings of Others

When you are so focused on achieving a goal and determined to succeed, it is easy to forget other things and become sidetracked. We have talked at length in our first chapter about how one of the main weaknesses of an ENTJ personality type is a lack of emotional understanding.

Before we get into the real crux of the issue, it's important to point out that as an ENTJ, we are not accusing you of becoming a cold-hearted ice king or queen, someone who never thinks about the feelings of others, because this isn't the case. As an ENTJ, you are simply not as in tune with your emotions as someone who is more of an introvert. We are all different, but focusing on improving our weaknesses is the way to success. Instead, we are suggesting that if you can learn to be more understanding and tolerant of the feelings of others, whilst also getting in touch with your own, you could develop yourself to an even higher level. That's really what this journey is all about! You love growth, and this journey is certainly going to tick that box for you.

Because you are more logical in the way you think, and you are fantastic at that strategic problem solving we mentioned earlier, that means that anything which is emotionally charged doesn't really make any sense to you in terms of success. An ENTJ doesn't get the job done by the force of their emotions, they get the job done by the force of their actions. This is how you are likely to be thinking, so why would you need to change a recipe that already works? Well, because sometimes more than one way of acting and thinking is the best course of action.

Now, when you are dealing with team members, customers, clients, and anyone else around you who is more of an emotional personality type, someone who is very in tune with their feelings, then you can sometimes become frustrated and annoyed with what you perceive to be their lack of action. The truth is that they are not lacking in action, it is just their way to be more laid back about things. The ironic thing here is that if you can learn to also be a little more laid back, just a tad. Then you may find even more creative solutions to problems!

The first step in becoming more tolerant of the feelings of those around you is to become a little more in tune with your own. We all have feelings, they are part of being a human being, and you have them too. But you simply don't feel they make that much logical sense. This isn't to say you never feel sad, angry, happy, or joyful, because the sheer feeling of determination is an emotion in itself! We're going to talk in a later chapter about how to achieve a better home and work-life balance, but it really is about taking time out for yourself and really learning to listen to the way you feel. You spend so much time working, so much time trying to focus on success, that you don't listen to your intuition in a way that isn't based on facts. Not everything in life, and even in business, has to make logical sense.

Learn to realize that it is okay to feel tired, to feel angry, to feel sad, upset, jealous, or even simply like you just don't want to do anything that particular day. Feelings are not a failing, they are a strength. If you can harness the power of your emotions and weave it into your fantastic drive and determination then you will become someone whom there can be no stopping!

Understanding Your Team Members

Part of being an ENTJ is about being a fantastic leader, but being a leader isn't all about inspiration, action, and speeches, it is about understanding your team members too. Learn to see beyond the job, and learn to really look at your team members. Do any of them seem a little off their game? Do any of them seem lacking in energy? Do any of them seem like something is bothering them? Life has a habit of getting us down from time to time, and a stressful existence is not a healthy one.

So, how can you learn to be a little more in tune with your own emotions, in order to be more tolerant and recognizing of those around you?

- Give yourself some time off and do the things you enjoy outside of your work
- Accept your feelings as being valid

- When you are given a solution by a team member which is more emotionally focused, do not throw it one side. Instead, give it the time of day by exploring whether it may actually work
- Turn negatives into positives
- Every morning, take five minutes to really explore the way you are feeling. Do you feel tired? Do you feel happy? Are you angry about something? Identifying whether an underlying issue is bothering you is a healthy way to live, and it will always be your emotions which are the first sign of this
- Get outdoors and enjoy Mother Nature
- Make exercise a regular part of your working week
- Ensure you are looking after yourself, e.g. you are getting enough sleep, you are eating healthily etc...
- Try yoga. This is fantastic for turning your thoughts inwards, and is also great for stress relief

By becoming more in tune with the way you are feeling personally, you will be able to recognize the emotional needs of your team members much more easily. The ironic thing is that by doing this, you will become a much more inspirational and greater leader as a result, which is only a good thing for future success.

4

Learn to Achieve a Home/Work-Life Balance

We have some news for you - you are allowed to have some time off! You need to have some time off! You need to give yourself 'you' time!

As an ENTJ you are super-focused and doggedly determined, and we have highlighted several times that this is a very enviable personality trait to have. The downside of that is that you can often become so wrapped up in work or the issue at hand, that you forget that downtime and time off overall are just as important. You may have a family or partner, or you may not. But whether you do or not, the fact remains that for your soul, your health, your wellbeing, as well as your success rate, you need to rest from time to time!

As an energetic and hard-working person, it is understandable that you want to make sure all that effort comes to fruition, but what is the point of anything if at the end of the day you go home half-asleep, too tired to spend any time with your children, too exhausted to sit and have a general chat with your partner, or too wiped out to even eat your dinner? For that reason, it is vital as an ENTJ that you understand the importance of having a little time for yourself too.

What a home and work-life balance is to you personally really depends on your circumstances. It depends on whether you have children, a partner, a family, any other commitments outside of work, etc... This also includes your circle of friends, because they are just as important too! By achieving balance, you really can have it all, and you won't be all too much one way or the other, e.g. too much work, not enough play, or too much play and not enough work (although that is highly unlikely with your personality type!). Learn to enjoy the fruits of your hard work – you deserve it!

There are a few ways you can try to achieve that home and work-life balance:

- **Always leave the office at a reasonable time** - It's understandable that as someone who is a leader you don't want to be leaving early, or always on time, but a reasonable hour is vital. Burning the midnight oil in order to meet a deadline or come up with a strategic solution to an issue is just going to lead to burn out, and that is not a road you want to be going down. We will talk more about that little gem a little later on.

- **Give yourself at least one day off per week** – As a team leader, you should always have a deputy that you trust. You are of course someone who is fantastic at identifying fresh, new talent, so why not groom your successor very early? Choose a deputy who can pick up the reins when you give yourself that all important one day off per week. Of course, two is better, but let's start off slowly! During that day off, do not check your work emails, do not answer any work calls, and do not call work either! This is going to be difficult for you at first, that is very understandable, but learning how to switch off occasionally is vital if you want to allow yourself to live a rich life outside of your work.

- **Always make time for friends and family** – You can often get so bogged down into a challenge, or with chasing a success, that you can forget to spend the right amount of time with those who are important to you. For that reason, always make time for them. Perhaps dedicating that one day off per week for a family day, and have a night off with your partner every week, where you have a date night. Have friends around to your house for dinner as a regular occurrence, and simply make sure that you check in with those important people in your life on a regular basis.

- **Find a hobby that you enjoy, and which inspires you** – We know that you love to succeed, and this is not just about work, it covers every facet of your life. Find yourself a hobby which distracts you from stress and any issues in your life, and which you can enjoy. So, it could be joining a sports team, it could be building a model railway, it could be renovating your home, it basically can be anything which you find interesting and challenging, and of course, enjoyable. Life goes by way too quickly. We often lose track of important hobbies and past times, because life gets in the way. Spend a little time to think about what you'd love to do.

As you can see, the advice isn't brain surgery level, but it can be something which is hard for an ENTJ to implement easily. You have an active mind, you are someone who doesn't like to rest, you always want to be achieving greatness somewhere along the line. What you need to realize is that by looking after number one, and having a harmonious balance in your life, you will give yourself the tools and energy to really push yourself to greater success in all areas of your life. If we cannot give ourselves a little time to relax, de-stress, and have fun, then how can we be our best for others in our lives?

The Dangers of Burnout

Even the greatest business minds in the world are human. Burnout/stress is a very real problem in today's fast-paced world, and it is something which an ENTJ is very susceptible to. The worrying problem is that as an ENTJ, you are so focused on success and logic, that you don't place much importance on your wellbeing and emotions. Your body and mind could be screaming at you to take a break, but you are so full of mental energy and determination that you just won't stop.

Stress is so worrying because it can be fatal in the worst-case scenarios. Did you know that stress can cause high blood pressure, which can then increase the chances of a stroke or heart problems? These are

22

not roads you want to go down. Stress is also a huge factor in anxiety and depression. An ENTJ may have trouble admitting to themselves that they are having problems like this, and if you suffer from this kind of situation, it might be that you see it as a weakness. The truth is that it is not a weakness, it is your body and mind telling you to slow down for a while! Without health, we have nothing.

Learn to listen to your body, and implement that home and work life balance we were just talking about. Even the world's biggest organizations, such as Microsoft and Google all understand this very real issue and put into place relaxation and wellness facilities for their staff. Take their lead and do the same for yourself.

5
Learn to Take a Step Back

This next chapter follows on seamlessly from our last one in many ways. An ENTJ is focused on success, we have said this many times, but there is also another side to the equation. A key trait of an ENTJ on the weakness side, is a tendency towards arrogance. We are not suggesting that as an ENTJ you are in any way a control freak, because it is actually much more about your will and determination, but to the outside world, it can appear to be about arrogance first and foremost.

Grabbing hold of the reins on whatever venture you are pouring yourself into so tightly can affect that home and work life balance we were just talking about, in fact, it makes it downright impossible to achieve. Allowing others to take charge from time to time, delegating tasks that don't require your attention, and understanding that it is okay to back off a little occasionally, will mean that you can not only look after yourself, your health and wellbeing, but also ensure that you are at your sharpest in order to achieve whatever it is you're working towards.

The problem in this regard? Trusting another worker or team member enough to be able to let go of the reins. We did touch upon this in our last chapter, and that as an ENTJ you are the master of the ship, you steer it in the direction it wants to go. This means that you also pick who is in your crew, and you are fantastic at identifying those who are true leaders for the future, and those who have skills which can really enhance whatever venture it is you're working towards. This also means that you can choose one of those team members to be someone who acts as your deputy during times when you need to back off a little, either for personal reasons, or because another task or issue is demanding your time.

You cannot do it all.

ENTJs often have an inability to be able to admit that they are overworked because they don't understand the concept! Of course, this is an admirable trait in many ways, because it means you are a true hard worker, someone who doesn't give up at the first sign of problems. The downside is that you cannot split yourself into several pieces, and you can only be in one place at once. If you spread yourself too thin then you risk only giving a portion of your attention to a project, and this is something which you are not at all happy to do. Having a deputy, someone you trust and can work with closely, means that you can focus your attention on areas that really require your specialist skills, whilst delegating the 'lesser' tasks, or the monitoring, to others.

Another point of learning to take a step back is that you might be able to come up with a new strategic answer to a problem. This allows you to have a little space, and to see things from a new perspective. The ability and drive to succeed really does come high upon the list of ENTJ traits, but sometimes being in the middle of a situation can be blinding. Take a step back and evaluable from outside, and you may just be able to achieve greater success, by seeing things much more clearly.

You Are The Navigator of Your Own Ship

As an ENTJ you love to be in the heart of the action, succeeding and finding ways to push yourself to even greater gains. This is fantastic, but learning to be a sailor, a captain, will also do you good. We talked in our last chapter about stress and burnout, and if you are trying to do everything then you will find that you are much more at risk of this happening to you. If you end up side-lined because of this issue then there's going to be no success coming your way! Learning to take this risk seriously is therefore vital.

Now, if you change your role slightly to be an overseer, i.e. someone who directs and pushes the boat in the right direction, encouraging and inspiring your crew to reach a common aim, then you will not only avoid these pitfalls, but the chances are that you will achieve much greater success as a result.

ENTJs are fantastic at inspiring other team members, even though they don't even realize it at the time. Look at the people you work with currently, do you feel they respect you? Do you feel they look up to you? Do you think they are inspired by your drive and hard work? Of course they are! This is because as a great leader you lead by example. Allowing yourself to remain with a few fingers in each pie, so to speak, but also allowing others to start their development journey, by letting go of the reins a little, means that you can become a mentor, as well as an inspiration. Again, ironically, this means your business success is also much more likely.

6
Learn to Harness The Power of Your Determination

Throughout this book, we have given a lot of attention to the fact that as an ENTJ you are a success story in the making, or already one published. You are someone who works hard and never gives up. We have highlighted the potential pitfalls in this, but how can you ensure that your hard work doesn't fail? How can you maximise that determination by really harnessing its power for good?

Identifying your personality type and then going on your own self-discovery journey isn't all about looking at your weaknesses and changing them, it is about enhancing the positives too! ENTJs are determined to the point of extremes sometimes. And whilst we know that you need to back off a little occasionally, for your own health and wellbeing, how can you really maximise that determination to help make yourself one of the greatest success stories around?

Let's look at Bill Gates for a second. This man invented Microsoft, the one innovation that every single person who has ever owned a computer has used at least once (and probably thousands) of times. This is a man who had a vision and worked tirelessly to make it work. Did he do it all on his own? No. Bill Gates recognized the potential in others, a key

ENTJ trait, and inspired them through his own innovation and hard work, to be a key part of his merry band of technological inventors. Gates is married, he has children, and manages to balance his home and work life, because he identified those team members that he could trust.

You are an ENTJ, just like Bill Gates. Your story could be equally as spectacular. Barack Obama – former President of the United States of America, one of the most determined yet personable men on the planet. Obama has a loving family, he found the balance that we were talking about two chapters ago, and he enlisted the help of his equally determined wife, Michelle Obama, to make their endeavors successful, even after the presidency finished.

What are we getting at here? We are talking about knowing you are determined, but finding ways to push that along, without getting too lost in the moment. Let's explore a few ways you can do this.

- Find the right people to work alongside you
  We've mentioned this already, but it is such a vital part of not only being an ENTJ, but also in life's successes too - identifying those who can help you grow and succeed, whilst also allowing themselves to develop at the same time. Use your keen eye for potential to identify the right people to work with you, and develop your team of like-minded, determined people. Having a harmonious work ethic, with everyone pulling in the same direction, at the same level, is key to an ENTJ, and key to success overall. You will be

inspiring others to work to the same standard as you, and that is a great thing.

- Find your real partner in life
Let's repeat the example we just gave about Barack Obama and his wife, Michelle. These two go together like the stars and the moon, because they are true partners in life, as well as in business. When searching for your ideal life partner, look for the same qualities you would do in a worker, but remember to allow your emotional side to develop and shine through too. This will truly give you the best of both worlds. This is one suggestion, but you may find you prefer having an opposite partner in a romantic relationship, which is fine. They main key is to find someone who you can be 100% yourself around. Someone who is willing to be by your side and support you. But most importantly, someone who makes you feel good.

- Understand when it is time to let go and move your eggs into another basket
You are doggedly determined - this is a truth. But it is also important to know that sometimes, things just don't work out. In order to really use your determination, you need to be aware that some things are best letting go of or changing them to work towards another avenue. Don't fall foul of flogging a dead horse, so to speak, when you could be investing your time into something more lucrative and more successful. Use your strategic thinking here.

- Maintain your sense of humor
  At all times, remember to keep that sense of humor! Look at Jim Carrey, a man who can laugh at himself more than most. He is an ENTJ, and a very successful man. Maintaining a true sense of being able to laugh at yourself during hard times, and to relieve stress is important in life. If you can't laugh at yourself and the situation around you, then you are too serious, and you are forcing yourself down a road that could possibly to a stressful and depressed state of being. Laugh and lighten the mood, and you will find yourself with a renewed sense of vigor, which will take you far.

- Plan and strategize to find the best avenue to go down
  You are a fantastic strategic thinker, but you do sometimes have the tendency to get a little over-excited about an idea and jump right in. Pull back that slight risk by brainstorming and working through every single thought avenue before you jump. Ask your team for their input, and take a step back to see things from the outside too.

- Don't rush - allow everything to work out in its own time
  We have talked about the fact that ENTJs are not known for their sensitivity, and that in some cases they can be a little akin to slight control freaks. Allowing a situation to pan out naturally, rather than forcing it, will allow you to see new

and innovative ways to solve problems. Looking at things from their natural point-of-view, rather than a constantly planned out point-of-view, can help you enhance your business or idea further, and give your determination something else to grab onto!

If you can use that fantastic and dogged determination and enhance it, you really are looking at Bill Gates-style success, or whatever success means to you.

7

Learn to See Relationships as Less of a Goal

Now it's time to get personal. We have talked at length about business so far in this book because this is what an ENTJ focuses on most, as well as general success in life. What you need to ask yourself at this point is how you look at friendships and romantic relationships.

When an ENTJ meets a new prospective partner, they have a tendency to look at whether this relationship is going to go the whole distance or not, and they do this very quickly. That, of course, means that they are not allowing the natural relationship to pan out, and who knows where it could lead if they simply took a step back and slowed down a little?

Does this sound like you?

It's important to recognize that all relationships, good or bad, offer us an opportunity to grow. They also reflect our own inner world. So, if you don't necessarily consider someone as a potential long-term partner, it doesn't necessarily mean that they aren't good in the short term. But this is something that only you can decide, based on knowing what you do or don't want.

This doesn't only relate to romantic relationships either, because it can also apply to new friendships. Success in life on all levels is vital to an ENTJ, and that means reaching an end goal. The problem with that mindset is that romance, in particular, is not about reaching a milestone destination, it is about growing with another person and experiencing life's ups and downs. There is no success other than simply being happy with that person. The same can be said for friendships, it is about finding support and solace in another like-minded person, to face life's adversities together.

As an ENTJ, it is likely that at the start of a new relationship, you are excited and someone who is always making plans. This is great because your partner is never bored, but it can also be overwhelming too. If you have picked someone who is more sensitive and emotionally-focused, then, of course, they are going to find this attention and perceived future plan very attractive and safe. But if you pick someone who is a bit more cautious and less likely to be emotionally-focused, then this could force them to run for the hills.

This can all be avoided by simply chilling the hell out in matters of the heart, and allowing things to come to the fore naturally. The greatest things in life cannot be planned, they evolve in their own way, and they often lead to the most wonderful destinations, if you only have the patience to wait it out. Patience is not your biggest strength as an ENTJ, but it is something you can hold onto and work towards. By doing so, your life will improve.

Another potential issue with relationships and the ENTJ is that if that person feels there is no success to be had in the partnership, they will simply cut their losses and move on, to find someone who they gel with in future plans better. Now, this can be upsetting for the other person, particularly if they are of the sensitive type. For that reason, it is vital that you, as an ENTJ, really think about what you want in a partnership, before going out there to find it. It is also a good idea to do a little of the emotional work we were talking about earlier in the book, because that will certainly help you gain much more of an open feel, and therefore give you a much better chance of meeting someone who not only meets your intellectual needs, but your deeply hidden emotional ones too.

This is all really about finding some common middle ground. For example, if you find yourself attracted to someone who is more in tune with their feelings than you are, but you find it rather odd that they don't think in the same way as you, turn that around and think for a second how they view you. Do you think they are perplexed by your sometimes cold exterior, or do you think they are trying to get under the surface a little? The chances are that the latter is correct, because they can see a wonderfully emotionally-connected person itching to get out! Find some middle ground and allow yourself to be vulnerable from time to time, and you will see your personal relationships grow into something that you not only see as success, but something which can be a sanctuary to you outside of your busy work life too.

Overall, this particular chapter really ties in well with our chat on becoming more in touch with your emotions, so it is worthwhile re-reading back over that content, to get a firmer grip on what we are trying to put over to you here. We have talked about how emotions are the biggest sticking point for an ENTJ, so be sure to put more time into this issue on your self-discovery journey.

8
Conclusion

And there we have it! You now know that as an ENTJ personality type, you are a true go-getter in life, and someone who is quite likely to succeed to a high level, through your real grit and determination. Your dogged, never say die spirit is admirable, and something which many other types look upon with jealousy, but it's important to remember that you have faults too! These faults, however, can be mended easily with a little mindset changing and working on yourself; the fact you have picked up this book shows an enviable desire to do just that.

ENTJs thrive on criticism to a large degree because they see it as a route towards growth and further success in the future. Take the content we have talked about in this book and use it as a tool to push you further forward. If anyone can do it, it's you!

As we mentioned at the very start of this book, it is likely that you display traits from surrounding personality types too, and that means looking into those types and digging out the relevant information. Regardless of whether you show the whole array of traits, or just one or two, it's really important to learn about the different personality types out there. Doing so will help you better understand and relate to others; people who don't think in the same way as you. This, of course, is a great way to help you further develop your leadership and management skills, because by understanding your team, you can push your joint endeavors towards achievement – something you love to do!

The major sticking point with an ENTJ personality is, of course, a tendency to come across as sometimes brutal with your feedback, and displaying a lack of emotion. You are not an emotional person by type, but that doesn't mean you can't learn to open up and tap into your emotions, to help develop yourself overall. This is going to be your biggest challenge out of all the advice we have given you so far. Give yourself time, and don't push it too much all at once. You are not born as someone who can talk easily about the way you feel, and you were not born someone who understands a more emotionally focused person – that's not to say you can't learn!

Use everything in this book as a source of future growth, and only then can you really be a force that can not only be reckoned with, but also someone who is influential and inspiring to others. If you feel you need further tuition on a certain part, don't hesitate to go back over another section and re-read it. The advice and exercises we have given you are designed to get you thinking about the issue, and then put it all into place to help you develop yourself further.

Note from the author

Thank you for purchasing and reading this book. If you enjoyed it or found it useful then I'd really appreciate it if you would post a short review on Amazon. I do read all the reviews personally so that I can continually write what people are wanting.
If you'd like to leave a review then please visit the link below:

https://www.amazon.com/dp/B076ZXQBNN

Thanks for your support and good luck!

Check Out My Other Books

Below you'll find some of my other books that are popular on Amazon and Kindle as well. Simply search the titles listed below on Amazon. Alternatively, you can visit my author page on Amazon to see other work done by me.

ENFP: Understand and Break Free From Your Own Limitations

INFP: Understand and Break Free From Your Own Limitations

ENFJ: Understand and Break Free From Your Own Limitations

INFJ: Understand and Break Free From Your Own Limitations

ENTP: Understand and Break Free From Your Own Limitations

INTP: Understand and Break Free From Your Own Limitations

INTJ: Understand and Break Free From Your Own Limitations

ENTJ: Understand and Break Free From Your Own Limitations

ENFP: INFP: ENFJ: INFJ: Understand and Break Free From Your Own Limitations -- The Diplomat Bundle Series

OPTION B: F**K IT - How to Finally Take Control Of Your Life And Break Free From All Expectations. Live A Limitless, Fearless, Purpose Driven Life With Ultimate Freedom

63917705R00027

Made in the USA
San Bernardino, CA
20 December 2017